# ANGIE EARL'S

*Treasured*

# LION HOUSE
# RECIPES

*Sincerely yours,*
*Angie Earl –*

PUBLISHED BY
BOOKCRAFT
SALT LAKE CITY
1st Edition

WESTERN PRINTING CO.
Salt Lake City
Printed in the United States of America

Have you met Angie Earl?

May we present her—

## MRS. LON EARL

Who has personally assembled and tested all the food patterns herewith submitted.

Out from a multitude of friendly requests comes this hand-book of supreme recipes. She has selected the ones most often requested.

For more than ten years Angie Earl has been cateress for the Lion House Social Center, the home of Brigham Young. Part of her time at the Center is given to food managing for the famous Cafeteria. She has given the Lion House all the materials and instruction of her experience.

Angie Earl has the warm mellow spirit of the best Pioneers. This friendly "Something" is tasteable in every food pattern that she has made.

Of pure Scotch descent she is the holder of many authentic Scotch as well as early American recipes.

With that true Pioneer Spirit she has helped plan reunions, weddings, community dinners and all other kinds of special occasions. "How much of this—and how little of that—how many pounds"—Such have been the inquiries. Freely she has given of her time in helping Relief Society and L.D.S. Ward organizations with food problems.

YOU will fully appreciate this 1947 Centennial contribution.

To

My noble and beloved mother

CATHERINE RUSSELL HOOD

## "LAND OF THE PIONEERS
## UTAH – WE LOVE THEE!"

One hundred years! That is a long time to advance from covered wagons to modern ways.

Have you ever pondered the ways of our Pioneers relative to foods—preparation and production. Compare the advancement—then, go count your blessings. Sometimes you can't buy butter, lard or whipping cream. Too bad, certainly our Pioneers knew about such things. What daily bread were they given? The threat of starvation faced them constantly. No doubt they were often filled with bitter disappointment and ate the roots of sego lilies that they might have the strength of faith and strength of body to reach a place of freedom—religious freedom.

Never were they idle. Every part of living demanded so much in labor that they dared not partake of idleness. Members of Pioneer households were numerous, and the HOME MAKER SUPREME never dreamed of labor-saving devices that would someday bless her children and their children.

All human history has not produced a more cheerful, willing or industrious bit of humanity.

Through years of privation they lived! Did well and looked well to the needs of those within their fold. They founded a great empire—from a truly barren waste.

May a kind Providence that guided them, help us, to remain forever grateful for all their endeavor.

*". . . . no toil nor labor fear,*
*but with JOY wend your way."*

# TABLE OF CONTENTS

## No. 1

*The staff that stays them.*

## CORN BREAD WITH BACON

Sift and measure 1 cup of all purpose flour. Sift again with 3½ teaspoons of baking powder —1¼ teaspoons of salt—2½ tablespoons of sugar—add 1 cup of yellow corn meal. Blend thoroughly.

Slightly beat 1 egg—add 1 cup of milk and 4 tablespoons of melted shortening. Combine with the flour, stirring just enough to mix the two parts together.

Dice and fry 6 slices of bacon. Turn the bacon and bacon fat into an 8"x8"x2" pan. Spread over with corn bread mix and bake 45 minutes in 425° oven.

Serves eight.

*We have come a long way since the days of "Dutch" ovens and side pork.*

*Oh happy day! We have regulated ovens! We do not have to grind our own corn into meal.*

## No. 2

## POTATO ROLLS

In a mixing bowl dissolve one yeast cake in 1 cup of cool potato water—add 1 cup of mashed potato and ¼ cup of sugar, let stand one hour.

Beat into the sponge 1½ teaspoons salt—6 tablespoons of melted shortening—2 well beaten eggs—add 3 cups of sifted all purpose flour and knead well, add enough extra flour to make a soft dough.

Let it rise until double its bulk.

Roll out until ¼ inch thick—spread with creamed butter, cut with a small biscuit cutter. Place 2 with buttered sides together and put into well greased muffin tins.

Let stand 45 minutes and bake in 400° oven for 25 minutes.

Makes 30 Rolls.

## No. 3

## BUTTERMILK BISCUITS

Sift 2 cups of all purpose flour with 4 teaspoons of baking powder, 1 teaspoon of salt and 2 teaspoons of sugar.

Rub into flour with finger tips 3 tablespoons of shortening—add ¾ cup of buttermilk. Cutting or mixing into the flour with a case knife until the dough forms a ball in the bowl.

Drop with a teaspoon on a well greased baking sheet—one inch apart. Bake in 425° oven for 25 minutes. After the first ten minutes in the oven brush with melted butter.

Makes 16 small biscuits.

*The odor of fresh bread baking will give you something to dream about.*

## No. 4

## "MORMON" PANCAKES with SIDE PORK

Parboil 8 slices of salt pork—wipe dry and fry brown on both sides—take it from pan and keep it warm.

In a mixing bowl beat 2 eggs—add 2 cups of milk—add 2¼ cups of flour—sifted with 1 teaspoon of salt—1 teaspoon of sugar—4 teaspoons of baking powder. Beat well—then beat in 2 tablespoons of salt pork drippings.

Heat griddle pan and grease with the salt pork drippings. Bake to even brown. As each one is ready to come off the griddle—roll one slice of the fried pork into the cake. Trickle over it plenty of hot syrup.

## PIONEER SYRUP

Measure 1 cup of corn syrup into small sauce pan. Blend with it 2 tablespoons of molasses. Heat—but do not boil. If a thin syrup is desired add ¼ cup of water.

*The smouldering smell of sagebrush is all that is needed to make this a real pioner breakfast.*

## NO. 5

## SCOTCH SCONES

*Honey—you'll love it! Molasses or jam, too.*

In a mixing bowl sift 2 cups of all purpose flour, 1 teaspoon of salt, 1 teaspoon sugar, 1 teaspoon soda and 1 teaspoon of baking powder.

Rub into this mixture 4 tablespoons of butter—add 1 cup of buttermilk. Stir only enough to combine all the ingredients.

Separate dough into four pieces—rolling each piece into a six inch disk.

Heat griddle iron moderately hot, sprinkle it lightly with flour. Bake scones until well browned on both sides. Turn them only once.

Serve with butter and honey creamed together.

## No. 6

## ORANGE TEA ROLLS

Put on to boil ½ cup of water—⅓ cup of shortening and 3 tablespoons of sugar. When it comes to boil pour into mixing bowl—let stand until cool. Add 1 teaspoon of salt—1 yeast cake and 2 well beaten eggs—add gradually 3 cups of sifted flour and ½ cup of warm milk until it forms a soft dough. Kneed well and let stand 2 hours.

Roll out until the dough is ½ inch thick and about six inches wide. Spread with orange filling—roll as you would a jelly roll and cut into ½ inch slices. Place in well greased muffin tins. Let them rise 1 hour. Bake in 400° oven for 25 minutes.

### ORANGE FILLING

Cream well ½ cup of sugar—¼ cup of butter—2 tablespoons of grated orange rind.

## No. 7

## GINGER BREAD

*"Some like it hot—some like it cold"*

In mixing bowl beat 2 eggs with ½ cup of sugar—add 4 tablespoons of melted shortening—4 tablespoons of maple syrup—½ teaspoon of salt—⅓ teaspoon of ginger—¼ teaspoon of cloves—1 teaspoon of cinnamon—add ½ cup of sour milk.

Then add and mix well 1½ cups of all purpose flour sifted twice with ½ teaspoon of baking powder—½ teaspoon of baking soda and spread in shallow, well greased baking pan. Sprinkle over with 1 cup of chopped walnuts dusted with 1 teaspoon of cinnamon.

Bake 35 minutes in 325° oven.

## No. 8

## GRAHAM CRACKER, WHIPPED CREAM LAYER CAKE

Cream ½ cup of butter with 1 cup of brown sugar—add 3 egg yolks—beat 2 minutes. Alternate ¾ cup of milk with 3 cups of graham cracker crumbs that have been rolled very fine and mixed with 1½ teaspoons of baking powder —⅓ teaspoon of salt—add 1 teaspoon of vanilla and ½ teaspoon of almond flavoring. Blend well—then fold in the beaten egg whites. Pour in two 8"x10"x2" tins.

Bake 35 minutes in 375° oven.

Cool and frost between layers and over top and sides with whipped cream.

## No. 9

# MARBLE CAKE WITH BURNT BUTTER ICING

Beat 2 eggs until thick and lemon colored—gradually beat in 1 cup of sugar—sift together 1½ cups of all purpose flour with 1 teaspoon of salt—½ teaspoon of baking soda—⅛ teaspoon of nutmeg.

Add alternately with 1 cup of heavy sour cream and 1 teaspoon of vanilla.

Remove ⅓ of the dough to another bowl and add 1 ounce of melted Bakers chocolate with 3 tablespoons of sour cream.

Alternate spoonfuls of chocolate and white dough into a well buttered bake pan—8"x10"x2" and bake 45 minutes in a 350° oven. Cool and ice.

## BURNT BUTTER ICING

In a saucepan put ½ square of butter—place over direct heat and let cook to a dark brown. Remove from the stove and add 3 tablespoons of cream—1 teaspoon of vanilla and 1½ cup of powdered sugar. Beat until smooth and creamy and spread over cake.

*Families still celebrate with this special offering.*

## No. 10

## SUNSHINE CAKE DE LUXE

In a mixing bowl put the yolks of 7 eggs with 4 tablespoons of cold water. Beat until thick and lemon colored. Gradually add 1⅓ cups of sugar. Beat until it is thick and heavy—add ½ cup of boiling water and fold in 1⅓ cups of cake flour that have been sifted 3 times—add 2 teaspoons of vanilla.

Have ready 7 egg whites beaten to the gloss stage with 1 teaspoon of cream of tartar and ½ teaspoon of salt. Fold into egg yolk mixture. Pour into tube pan. Bake 1 hour in 275° oven— Remove from oven and invert the pan. Let it stand 1 hour.

Serve with whipped cream and maraschino cherries.

*Sunshine, anytime!*

## No. 11

## GINGER CAKE

Cream ½ cup of butter with ½ cup and 2 tablespoons of sugar—add 2 well beaten eggs—add ½ cup of molasses—2½ cups of flour sifted with 1½ teaspoons of soda—¾ teaspoon of ginger—1 teaspoon of cinnamon—½ teaspoon of salt—1 cup of hot water.

Beat well and bake in shallow pan 35 minutes in 350° oven.

Serve with whipped cream or custard sauce. Serves 15.

## CUSTARD SAUCE

In top of double boiler beat 2 eggs with ¾ cup of sugar sifted with 2 tablespoons of corn starch and ¼ teaspoon of salt—add 1½ cup of milk.

Place over boiling water and cook until thick and creamy. Stir constantly—add flavoring.

No. 12

## DE LUXE ICE BOX CAKE

Cream well ½ pound of butter with 3 cups of powdered sugar. Beat in 4 eggs—one at a time.

Drain well 1-#2 can of grated pineapple. Whip 1½ cups of cream.

Roll into fine crumbs 1 pound of vanilla wafers.

Spread evenly half of the crumbs in an 8"x10" cake pan (shallow)—Spread the butter mixture over the crumbs—then scatter the drained pineapple over the butter—then the whipped cream. Cover over with the vanilla wafer crumbs.

Place in refrigerator over night. Cut into 2x 2½ inch squares. Serve on a small plate—top with whipped cream and chopped nuts.

## No. 13

## GRANDMOTHER RUSSELL'S SCOTCH SHORT CAKE

Blend together 1 pound of butter and 1 pound of pure leaf lard. Onto a mixing board sift 3 pounds of flour—¾ pound of sugar, granulated, and ½ pound of powdered sugar.

Knead in the butter and lard adding a little at a time ½ pound more of flour. It must be worked until it is the consistency of putty. Then mold it into flat round 4 inch cakes about ½ inch thick. Keep the edges pressed together with fingers. Place each cake on a heavy brown paper and bake on cookie sheet in 300° oven for ½ hour.

If you wish to decorate them top each one with candy trim, caraway seed or sugar crystals, **before** placing in the oven.

## No. 14

## PRIZE CUP CAKES

*The house will be filled with a spiced aroma—
and little folk filled with glee!*

Cream well ½ cup of butter with 1 cup of sugar—add 2 well beaten eggs—alternate ¾ cup of milk with 1¾ cups of all purpose flour that have been sifted twice with 2 teaspoons of baking powder ½ teaspoon of salt and ½ teaspoon of mace. Add 2 teaspoons of vanilla flavoring. Fill well buttered muffin tins ⅔ full. Bake in 400° oven 25 minutes. While still warm remove from tins and brush entire cake with melted butter then roll in granulated sugar.

No. 15

## CHOCOLATE SPONGE CAKE

*Most unusual!*

Sift—then measure 1½ cups of cake flour—add 1½ teaspoons of baking powder—½ teaspoon of salt—sift together 4 times.

Cut fine ½ bar of baking chocolate—put in a sauce pan with 1 cup of milk. Place over heat and stir constantly until smooth and creamy. Cool.

Into a mixing bowl break 6 eggs—beat until thick and lemon color. Add, a little at a time, 2 cups of sugar, beat until well blended. Add 2 teaspoons of vanilla then add the cooled chocolate mixture. Fold in flour—pour in tube pan and bake 1 hour. Start heat at 275°—after 30 minutes turn heat control to 350°—invert pan and let stand 1 hour. Remove from pan and cover with seven minute icing.

## No. 16

## CHOCOLATE BOSTON CREAM PIE

Follow the chocolate sponge cake receipe (No. 15).

Instead of using the tube pan divide the batter into 3 layer cake pans. Bake in 300° oven for 25 minutes. Cool cake in the pans then split each layer using a saw bread knife. Put Boston Cream between each layer and top with whipped cream—sprinkle the top of cream with grated sweet chocolate.

## BOSTON CREAM FILLING

In the top of the double boiler put 3 cups of whole milk—½ square butter—⅔ cup of sugar —⅛ teaspoon of salt. When it comes to the scald point—thicken with ½ cup of corn starch moistened in 1 cup of milk. Stir until smooth and creamy.

Separate 3 eggs—beat yolks until thick and lemon colored. Pour hot mix over them and return them to double boiler. Place over the heat —let cook for 5 minutes. Beat the egg whites to the gloss stage—add ¼ cup of sugar. Pour the hot filling over the egg whites and fold the two mixtures together. Add 2 teaspoons of vanilla and cool. Divide the filling between the three cakes.

Serves 24.

## No. 17

## MOTHER HOOD'S FRUIT CAKE

Cream well 1 pound of butter with 1 pound of sugar—add 1 dozen eggs, one at a time, beating well into the butter and sugar as each egg is added.

Sift together 3 times—1 pound of flour—1 teaspoon of baking soda—½ teaspoon of salt—1 teaspoon of allspice—2 teaspoons of vanilla—½ teaspoon of lemon flavoring—½ teaspoon of almond flavoring. Add to the creamed mixture.

Add the fruit and nuts which have been prepared the night before. Combine thoroughly.

How to prepare the fruit and nut mixture:
Wash and dry well 2 pounds of seedless raisins—2 pounds of chopped seeded raisins—½ pound of lemon peel sliced very thin—½ pound of orange peel sliced very thin—½ pound of citron peel sliced very thin—1 pound of broken walnut meats—1 pound of pecan halves—2 cups of candied cherries.

Bake in loaf tins lined with cookie crust.

How to prepare cookie crust is given on the next page.

## No. 18

## COOKIE CRUST ALA MOTHER HOOD

Sift 3 cups of flour with 1 cup of sugar—1 teaspoon of baking powder—½ teaspoon of salt —2 teaspoons of cinnamon.

Rub into the dry ingredients until a fine con- sistency —1 cup of butter—mix in 1 cup of water until a stiff dough is formed.

Roll out very thin and line 5 well buttered loaf tins.

Press the cake mixture well into the corners. Cover the top with crust rolled and cut to fit the pans. Press edges together with a folk. Trim off all edges. Prick the entire top surface of the crust with a fork.

Set oven at 200° and bake for 1 hour—in- crease the heat to 225° for 2 hours. (Baking time 3 hours).

## COOKING MUST BE A LABOR OF LOVE

Once upon a time Luther Burbank declared that a meal prepared by a person who loves you will do more good than the average cooking—and on the other side of it a person who dislikes you is bound to get that dislike into your food without intending to.

Pioneer cooks knew about that—theirs was a kindly touch.

## No. 19

## CHEESE OMELET

Beat 5 eggs—add 3 cups of milk and 1 cup of canned milk—add 1½ teaspoons of salt—1 teaspoon of onion salt—⅛ teaspoon of pepper.

Stir until well blended. Pour into a well buttered casserole. Sprinkle over with ¼ pound of grated cheese. Dot with bits of butter and bake uncovered 1 hour in a 350° oven.

Serves ten.

## No. 20

## MACARONI AND CHEESE

Boil until tender 1½ cups of small cut macaroni in 1 quart of salted water. Drain and rinse well in cold water.

Grate 1½ cups of nippy cheese—butter heavy the sides and botton of a casserole.

Place half of the macaroni in the casserole sprinkle with half the grated cheese. Add the balance of the macaroni—then cheese.

Beat 1 egg slightly—add 1 quart of milk—1 teaspoon of salt—½ teaspoon onion salt and a dash of pepper.

Pour over the macaroni and cheese. Cover with buttered bread crumbs. Bake 1 hour in 300° oven.

Serves twelve.

## No. 21

## FRIED CHEESE BALLS

*To enhance that special ham dinner.*

Mix well 2 ounces of grated nippy cheese—1½ cups of soft bread crumbs—a few grains of cayenne pepper—⅓ teaspoon of onion salt and 2 egg yolks. Form into balls the size of a walnut—fry to a golden brown in butter.

# PIONEERS

*"They cut desire into short lengths*
*And fed it to the hungry fires of courage.*
*Long after—when the flames had died*
*Moulten gold gleamed in the ashes.*
*They gathered it into bruised palms*
*And handed it on to their children ·*
*And their children's children—forever."*

VILATE RAILE

## No. 22

## CHOCOLATE ICE BOX COOKIES

Cream together 1½ cups of butter with 1¼ cup of sugar—add 3 eggs—one at a time—add 3 tablespoons of cream—1 tablespoon of vanilla flavoring—add 4 cups of all purpose flour that have been sifted 3 times with 1 teaspoon of soda —½ teaspoon of salt and ¼ teaspoon of nut-meg. Add 4 squares of melted baking chocolate —press into loaf tin that has been lined with heavy wax paper. Place in refrigerator over night. Unmold and cut into 4 inch slices—cut each slice into ¼ inch strips. Place on buttered cookies sheet and bake 12 to 15 minutes in 300° oven.

*Dainties—to set before the village queens*

## No. 23

## BUTTER ALMOND COOKIES

Cream together 1 pound of butter—1 cup of sugar—add 2 well beaten eggs—add 4½ cups of all purpose flour that have been sifted 4 times with 1 teaspoon of soda and ½ teaspoon of salt. Add 1 teaspoon of almond flavoring—1 cup of finely chopped almonds.

Press into a wax paper lined cake pan (8"x8" and shallow)—place in refrigerator over night. Remove from pan—cut into 6 strips and cut each strip into thin slices. Place on buttered cookie sheet. Bake 10 to 12 minutes in 375° oven.

Makes about 175 cookies.

*So good for a small "sprize" in a packed lunch.*

## No. 24

## CARMEL ICE BOX COOKIES

Cream together 1 cup of butter with 1 cup of brown sugar—add 2 well beaten eggs—add 2½ cups of flour sifted 3 times with 1 teaspoon of soda—1 teaspoon of cinnamon—1 teaspoon of nutmeg and ½ teaspoon of salt. Add 1 teaspoon of vanilla—¼ teaspoon of maplene flavoring and 1 cup of chopped walnuts.

Divide the dough into 6 pieces—roll each piece into round sticks about 1½ inches thick—roll each stick in wax paper—place in the refrigerator over night.

Cut each stick into thin slices—place on buttered cookie sheet and bake 15 minutes in 325° oven.

Makes about 125 cookies.

*Simple and simply charming.*

## No. 25

## MOLASSES COOKIES

Cream ½ cup of sugar with ¼ cup of shortening—add 1 beaten egg—½ cup of molasses —1 tablespoon of vanilla.

Sift together 2¼ cups of flour with ½ teaspoon of ginger—1 teaspoon of nutmeg—½ teaspoon of salt—1 teaspoon of soda. Add alternately the above mixture with ½ cup of buttermilk.

Drop by spoonfulls two inches apart on greased baking sheets and bake 12 minutes in 375° oven.

*Try these on rainy days—*

No. 26

## CHOCOLATE BROWNIE BARS

Cream together ⅓ cup of soft butter with ⅓ cup of Aunt Dinah's molasses—add 1 well beaten egg and 2 squares of melted baking chocolate—add 1 cup of all purpose flour that has been sifted three times with 1 teaspoon of baking powder—⅓ teaspoon of salt—add 1 cup of chopped nuts.

Line a shallow cake pan (8"x10") with heavy wax paper—spread the mixture evenly and bake 15 minutes in 325° oven.

Remove the paper from the cake as soon as it has been taken from the oven and cut cake into strips 1 inch wide by 2½ inches long or into 2 inch squares. Use a sharp knife.

*These can make any gathering a party.*

## No. 27

## ORANGE TEA STRIPS

Cream 5 tablespoons of butter with 1 cup of sugar—add 1 tablespoon of grated orange rind add 2 eggs, beat well after each egg. Add 2 cups of sifted cake flour with 2 teaspoons of baking powder and ¼ cup of top milk—⅓ cup of orange juice—½ teaspoon of lemon flavoring— ¼ teaspoon of salt.

Beat well and spread in a well buttered 12"x 15" baking pan. Spread on topping made as follows:

Beat 1 egg white stiff but not to the dry stage —fold in 4 tablespoons of sugar and a few drops of orange flavoring. Spread this over cake batter and sprinkle over with cocoanut, chopped nuts or candied cherries.

Bake 25 minutes in 300° oven. Cut into strips 2½ inches long and 1 inch wide.

## ORANGE MARSHMELLOW FLUFF

Whip 1 cup of cream—fold in ½ pound of marshmellows cut in small pieces—2 cups of diced orange—½ cup of broken nut meats.

Top squares of sunshine cake, butter cake or angel cake.

*". . . . 'tis better far for us to strive,*
*our useless cares from us to drive.*
*Do this—and joy your hearts will swell,*
*all is well. . . ."*

No. 28

## HALIBUT EN CASSEROLE

Tie in a cheese cloth 3 pounds of halibut—
(center cut). Simmer 1 hour in salted water—
drain well—discard all bone and skin. Flake
the halibut.

Make 1½ quarts of heavy rich white sauce.
Season with 1 teaspoon of salt—1 teaspoon of
onion salt—⅛ teaspoon of pepper. Butter heavy
the sides and bottom of casserole.

Pour 1½ cups of the white sauce in the bottom of the casserole. Add half of the fish that
has been flaked. Sprinkle over the fish 2 teaspoons of minced pimiento and ¼ cup of grated
cheese (mild nippy). Add 2 cups of white sauce
and repeat the fish, cheese and pimiento. Add
the balance of the white sauce—dot with butter
and bake 1 hour in 250° oven.

Serves fifteen.

## No. 29

## SALMON LOAF WITH EGG SAUCE

Boil 2 pounds of fresh salmon in salted water until it leaves the bone. Drain and cool. Flake the salmon discarding all the bone and skin.

Put in top of double boiler—1 quart of milk—cook over boiling water until it is at the scalding point—blend together—½ cup flour with ½ square of butter and one teaspoon of salt—add to milk and stir constantly until it cooks into a heavy white sauce.

Slowly fry ¾ cup of finely chopped onion in 3 tablespoons of butter. Combine in a mixing bowl the white sauce, salmon, onions, one cup of dried ground bread crumbs—¼ cup of lemon juice—1 teaspoon of salt—and a dash of pepper and 2 well beaten eggs. Mix well and pour into a well greased baking pan. Bake one hour in a moderate oven. Serve with egg sauce.

## EGG SAUCE

Make one pint of medium white sauce. Add 1 teaspoon of prepared mustard—½ teaspoon Worcestershire sauce—and 2 hard boiled eggs chopped.

Serves 14.

## No. 30

## DEVILED CRAB

In a sauce pan melt 4 tablespoons of butter—add 3 tablespoons of flour—1 teaspoon of Colman's dry mustard—1 teaspoon of salt—a dash of pepper. Blend well—then add 2 cups of milk and cook until smooth and creamy—add 2 tablespoons of lemon juice—1 tablespoon of chopped parsley—½ teaspoon of onion juice—2 chopped hard boiled eggs—1 cup of soft bread crumbs.

Combine well—then fold in 2 cups of fresh or canned crab meat. Place in a well buttered casserole—scatter buttered bread crumbs over the top.

Bake in 375° oven for 45 minutes.

Serve with tartar sauce.

No. 31

## HAM BISCUITS ON CREAMED TUNA

Make 1 quart of heavy white sauce—fry ⅓ cup of chopped onion—½ cup of celery chopped very fine in 3 tablespoons of butter until tender but not brown. Fold through the white sauce with 1 tablespoon of Worcestershire sauce and 1 cup of flaked, white, solid meat, tuna. Serve in ramikins topped with a ham biscuit.

### HAM BISCUIT

Sift into a mixing bowl 1½ cups of flour with 3 teaspoons of baking powder—½ teaspoon of salt—½ teaspoon of sugar. With the finger tips or pastry cutter blend in 3 tablespoons of shortening. Toss in 1 cup of finely chopped boiled ham. Add 1 cup of fresh butermilk. Roll out and cut with small biscuit cutter. Bake 25 minutes in 400° oven. Brush tops with butter.

## No. 32

## SALMON OMELET

Beat lightly 5 eggs—add 3 cups of milk and 1 cup of canned milk—1½ teaspoons of salt—a dash of pepper. Pour into well buttered casserole.

Fold in 2 cups of flaked cooked or canned salmon.

Dot with small bits of butter and bake 50 minutes in a 350° oven.

Serves eight.

## No. 33

## MEAT DISHES

## HAM SHORT CAKE

Combine 1 quart of heavy white sauce with 3 cups of ground cooked ham—1 cup of drained canned peas—2 teaspoons of grated onion. Mix well and pour into a well buttered 8"x10" baking pan.

Sift 2 cups of flour with 4 teaspoons of baking powder—1½ teaspoons of salt—2 teaspoons sugar. Blend in well 5 tablespoons of shortening. Cut in with a knife 1¼ cups of milk.

Place by spoonfulls over the ham in the pan and carefully spread over the entire surface. Brush with melted butter and sprinkle over with 1 cup of ground ham.

Bake in 400° oven for 50 or 60 minutes.

Will serve ten.

*Food preparation can show a kindly attitude.*

## No. 34

## SWISS STEAK

Select 2½ pounds of top round steak—1 inch thick—cut into 6 pieces—pound 2 tablespoons of flour into each piece of meat. Fry brown on both sides in deep fat. Slice 1 medium size onion in the bottom of a casserole with ½ of a bay leaf. Place meat on top of the onion—salt and pepper each piece of meat.

Drain all the fat from the frying pan—add 1 quart of water to the fryings left in the pan—add 1 teaspoon of salt—1 teaspoon of beef steak sauce—½ teaspoon of kitchen bouquet. Bring to a boil and pour it over the steak. Add enough water so the steak is completely covered.

Cover the casserole—cook 2 hours in 325° oven.

*Be happy with what you have to prepare, it will grow into successful achievement.*

## No. 35

## GOLDEN WEST STUFFED PORK CHOPS

Select 6 center loin pork chops 1½ inches thick. Wipe each with a damp cloth and remove all loose pieces of bone. Trim off any excess fat. With a sharp knife cut a deep pocket in each chop—put 1 tablespoon of stuffing in each pocket and fasten with a tooth pick.

Sprinkle each chop with salt and pepper and a few drops of lemon juice. Dredge with flour and let stand ½ hour. Dip in beaten egg—roll in fine bread crumbs and fry to a golden brown in deep fat. Place on a rack in a roaster. Add 1 cup of water. Bake 1 hour in 275° oven.

## STUFFING

Toss together 2 cups of soft bread crumbs— 2 tablespoons of finely chopped onions fried in 2 tablespoons of butter—¼ cup of grated apple —⅓ teaspoon of salt—a dash of pepper. Moisten with 3 tablespoons of canned milk.

## No. 36

## BRAIZED BEEF CUBES IN SAVORY SAUCE

In a roasting pan melt 4 tablespoons of fat. Put 4 pounds of sirloin beef cubes in and stir until each cube acquires some of the fat. Place in 450° oven. Sear for ½ hour. Add 1 quart of water with 1 teaspoon of salt—a dash of pepper. Cover the roaster and reduce oven heat to 325° —cook 1 hour longer then add the sauce—cooking until the meat is very tender.

Combine 1½ quarts of tomato juice—½ cup of catsup—1 tablespoon of kitchen bouquet—¼ teaspoon garlic salt—2 tablespoons of sugar— 1 teaspoon of salt—2 tablespoons of minced onion—¼ teaspoon of ground cloves.

No. 37

## CREAMED EGG WITH LIVER

Melt in the top of double boiler 1 tablespoon of butter—blend in 1 tablespoon of flour—⅓ teaspoon of salt—a bit of pepper. Stir in slowly 1 cup of top milk. Cook 15 minutes stirring frequently.

Add 2 hard cooked eggs that have been chopped.

Cover 1 pound of sliced liver with boiling water—let stand 5 or 10 minutes—drain well and broil or fry in fat until brown on both sides. Place in casserole. Cover with creamed eggs—bake 20 minutes in 375° oven.

Serves 6.

## No. 38

## VEAL CUBES SPECIALIZED

Brown 1 pound of 1 inch veal cubes with 3 tablespoons of minced onions in 3 tablespoons of shortening. Combine 2 cups of tomato puree and 3 cups of tomato juice. Add 1-8 ounce can of murshrooms—1 tablespoon of minced pimiento—1 teaspoon of salt—3 teaspoons of sugar —$\frac{1}{4}$ teaspoon of cloves—1 teaspoon of Worcestershire sauce—1 teaspoon of onion salt. Add the veal cubes and simmer 1 hour.

Thicken to consistency of thick cream.

Boil in salted water $1\frac{1}{2}$ cups of egg shellroni until well cooked. Drain and wash well—drain again. Combine with the veal cubes and simmer 10 minutes longer.

Will serve 12.

*"So good to come home to—"*

No. 39

## BAKED MEAT LOAF

Combine 1 pound of the best ground beef—
1 pound of ground lean pork—3 teaspoons of
salt—2 teaspoons of rubbed sage—¼ teaspoon
of pepper—2 teaspoons of Worcestershire sauce
—3 tablespoons minced onions—1 cup of corn
flakes—½ cup dried ground bread crumbs—2
cups of milk.

Mix well and press into a well greased loaf
pan.

Bake one hour in 350° oven.

Serves ten.

## No. 40

## LUNCHEON DELIGHT

Have your butcher slice for you 8 slices of boiled ham ⅛ of an inch thick. Spread each slice with any good cheese spread (the flavors can be changed). Roll up with the cheese inside. Place in a well buttered shallow baking pan. Bake in 350° oven for 20 minutes. Serve with a tablespoon of UTAH sauce.

## UTAH SAUCE

Make 1 quart of rich white sauce. Fold in 1 tablespoon of prepared mustard—2 hard boiled eggs grated—½ teaspoon of paprika.

*Delight your friends by serving this with a tossed green salad and hot buttermilk biscuits.*

No. 41

## BEEF WITH MACARONI

Boil until tender 1 cup of small cut egg maca-roni in 1 quart of salted water. Drain and rinse well in cold water.

Fry ½ cup of chopped onion and 2 table-spoons of chopped green pepper in 4 tablespoons of shortening. Combine in sauce pan—1 cup of tomato puree and 1 quart of tomato juice—1 tea-spoon of salt—1 tablespoon of sugar—½ tea-spoon of savory salt—a dash of pepper—1 table-spoon of vinegar. Add the macaroni and 1 pound of best ground beef fried until well browned. Simmer 1 hour.

Serves eight.

No. 42

## LAMB AND RICE CROQUETTES

### with

### CREAMED PEAS

Steam in a double boiler ⅓ cup of rice in 3 cups of water with 1 tablespoon of butter and ½ teaspoon of salt. Cook until fluffy.

Make a white sauce with 2 cups of lamb stock —2 cups of canned milk—thicken with ½ cup of flour blended with ½ square of butter—1 teaspoon of salt—a dash of pepper—½ teaspoon of rubbed garden sage.

Combine 4 cups of cooked ground lamb with the white sauce—rice and ½ cup of chopped fried onions. Chill over night.

Form into croquettes—roll in flour—dip in egg diluted with milk—roll in crumbs and pan fry in deep fat.

Serve them topped with creamed peas.

## No. 43

## WESTERN BAKED HAM WITH RAISIN SAUCE

Select a 12 pound ham (tenderized)—have the butcher take two pounds from the hock end— (sell that back to him or save it for your next bean dinner).

Wash the ham and cover with hot water— add ½ cup of vinegar—1 teaspoon of celery seeds—4 teaspoons of mustard seeds. Bring to a boil then turn heat down to simmer the ham— cook 2½ hours. Let cool in liquid—then place it fat side up in roaster pan—cut ½ inch deep lines criss cross in the fat—work into it 1 cup of brown sugar—sprinkle with 1 teaspoon of ground cloves—put 2 cups of the liquid the ham was boiled in, in the pan. Bake 1 hour in 325° oven.

Slice and serve with Raisin Sauce.

Raisin Sauce No. 68.

From pioneer days to days of luxury and indulgence, food has been just food. We dress it up differently. With what food is available we put together combinations—adding spices or flavorings and decorate it to please the eye.

All the way down the years we catch and try to hold, the spirit, as well as the ingenuity of our maternal pioneer parents. Blessed mothers they were—we have just added upon because we are blessed with an abundance of all good things of the earth.

Little Grandmother Baird carried six treasured recipes in the bosom of her dress as she trudged the many miles across the plains. True SHE could not produce the where-with-all to complete some of her treasured goodies. However, she knew, the day would come when she would have the necessary ingredients.

The day of planting did come—the earth yielded—and then the day of harvest. She was able to give her neighbors and their friends the benefit of those six treasures!

One of the six recipes was for chili sauce. It is found to be a great favorite even today. Would you like to have it? Here it is on the following page:

## No. 44

## CHILI SAUCE
## ALA GRANDMOTHER BAIRD

Scald and peel 1 peck of ripe tomatoes and put through a food chopper. Add 3 teacups of ground green peppers—2 teacups of ground onions—2⅔ teacups of sugar—⅓ teacup of salt—3 pints of vinegar—3 teaspoons of whole cloves—3 teaspoons of ground cinnamon—2 teaspoons of nutmeg—1½ teaspoons of ginger.

Bring to a rolling boil—then boil gently 4 hours. Stirring frequently. When ready to take from the stove add 1 gill of brandy and bottle.

## No. 45

## GREEN RELISH

Put through food chopper 1 peck of green tomatoes—12 large onions—3 green peppers— 3 sweet red peppers—3 pound head of white cabbage—add 2 quarts of cider vinegar—1 quart of sugar—3 tablespoons of salt—1 tablespoon of allspice—1 teaspoon of ground cloves—2 teaspoons celery seeds—2 teaspoons of white mustard seeds—2 teaspoons of tumeric.

Boil gently 40 minutes—then stir in ¼ cup of Coleman's mustard moistened in ½ cup of vinegar.

Seal while hot.

## No. 46

## BREAD AND BUTTER PICKLES

Slice 4 quarts of unpeeled, dill size, cucumbers. Peel 1½ quarts of very tiny pickling onions. Soak together over night in weak brine (2 quarts water with ¼ cup of salt.)

Drain and rinse well—cover with 1 quart of vinegar—1 cup of water—2 cups of sugar—2 teaspoons of tumeric—3 teaspoons of celery seeds—4 teaspoons of white mustard seeds—2 teaspoons of whole cloves.

Boil 20 minutes and seal in bottles.

## No. 47

### SWEET RED PEPPER RELISH

Put through food chopper 25 sweet red peppers—15 medium size onions. Cover with boiling water and let stand 15 minutes. Drain and cover with a solution of 1 pint vinegar and 1 quart water brought to a boil. Cover the mixture and let stand 15 minutes—then drain well.

Boil together 1 quart of vinegar—6 cups sugar —5 tablespoons of salt—3 tablespoons of mustard seed—1 teaspoon of celery seeds.

Pour over the mixture and bring to a boil. Bottle and seal.

*The house will be filled with spiced aroma, and your family filled with appetite!*

## No. 48

# CHOW CHOW WHEN COMPANY COMES

Put through the food chopper 1—3-pound head of hard white cabbage—6 extra large onions—20 large peeled cucumbers.

Cover with brine (1 gallon of water to ½ teacup of salt). Let stand over night—drain and cover with weak vinegar (2 parts vinegar to 1 part water) for two days. Drain well.

Peel ½ peck of tiny white pickling onions. Wash, stem 20 very small cucumbers (1 inch long). Wash and break into tiny flowerlets 2 pounds of cauliflower. Soak each vegetable separately for two hours in weak salt water. Drain —then cover each vegetable with fresh water and boil gently for ten minutes. Drain—then add to chopped vegetables. Add ½ pint of horseradish—2 ounces of white mustard seed— 1 teaspoon ground white pepper—½ ounce of celery seed. Mix well and place in a stone jar.

Boil 2½ quarts of white malt vinegar with 2 pounds of brown sugar—½ teaspoon of maplene flavoring. Pour boiling hot over the pickles for five mornings. Drain liquid from pickles—bring to a boil and pour over them— the fifth morning put the chow chow in a kettle and bring just to a rolling boil. Stir in ½ teacup of Colman's mustard—1 teaspoon of tumeric mixed to a thin paste with vinegar. Seal the bottles at once.

*A lot of work? Perhaps—but so very good!*

The following are delicacies only dreamed of in the days of 1847.

1947 Daughters of Utah Pioneers, with their culinary art, have especially requested these delightful foods.

## THAT FAMOUS PIE CRUST

Angie Earl gave to the Lion House Social Center this famous recipe. She received it from her Scotch mother, Catherine Russell Hood, who received it from her mother, Elsabeth Johnston Russell.

It is given you with the thought that you too, can excel in putting it together.

# THE FAMOUS—ANGIE EARL PIE CRUST

Sift into a mixing bowl 2 cups of all purpose flour—1 teaspoon of salt—1 teaspoon of sugar. With the finger tips break through the flour ⅔ square of butter into halfs inch bits. Then break in ¾ cup of lard making the pieces half the size of the butter bits.

With a case knife cut in ½ cup of ice water adding only a little at a time. When the dough forms into a ball turn it onto a floured board and knead just enough to have a smooth dough. Roll into double wax paper and let stand in refridgerator over night or longer if possible.

For best results have the butter and lard very cold. It may be kept in the fridge from 5 to 7 days.

This pie crust is especially fine for two-crust pies or pre-baked shells.

Because of its water content it requires longer baking time.

Preheat oven to 400°. After baking 20 minutes reduce heat to 350°.

## No. 49

*"By their fruits"*

### DEEP DISH APPLE PIE

Peel and slice very thin 4 cups of apples.

Blend together 1 cup of sugar—2 tablespoons of corn starch—½ teaspoon of cinnamon—⅛ teaspoon of salt and a few drops of lemon flavoring.

Sprinkle over the apples or toss them so all the apples are coated with some of the sugar mixture. Let stand one hour. Turn into well buttered baking pan 8"x8"x2" and cover with pastry crust rolled ¼ inch thick. Cut air hole in center to let steam escape. Press to all four edges of the pan. Dot with butter, sprinkle lightly with sugar and bake 1 hour. Start baking in 400° oven.

*Don't be sour when you feed hungry folk!*

Many food surprises can come from this pie
crust recipe—try cinnamon sticks, sometime.

No. 50

## PUMPKIN CUSTARD PIE

Into a mixing bowl put 1½ cups of canned or prepared pumpkin. Break into this 5 eggs—add 1½ cups of sugar sifted with ¼ cup of flour— 1 tablespoon of cinnamon—½ teaspoon of ginger—½ teaspoon of nutmeg—1 teaspoon of salt —1 teaspoon of vanilla flavoring—½ teaspoon of lemon flavoring and 1 tablespoon of Aunt Dinah's molasses.

Stir all together with a wire cake spoon until well blended. Then add 3 cups of milk—1 cup of canned milk—3 tablespoons of melted butter. Beat with a rotary egg beater just enough to combine all ingredients.

Pour into 3 pastry lined pie tins that have been chilled in the refrigerator for 1 hour.

Bake 15 minutes in 425° oven then reduce the heat to 325° and bake for 40 minutes more.

## No. 51

## GOOSEBERRY TARTS

Over shallow muffin tins—bake 12 individual tart shells. (See the pie crust recipe on the red page.)

### Filling

Wash and stem 2 cups of ripe gooseberries. Simmer them for 15 minutes with ½ cup of water in a sauce pan with a tight cover.

Add ¾ cup of sugar—3 tablespoons of butter —⅛ teaspoon of salt and a few drops of red food coloring.

Disolve 3 tablespoons of corn starch in water and carefully stir into the goosberries. Cook 1 minute—cool.

Add ⅓ teaspoon of lemon flavoring and 3 drops of almond flavoring.

Fill the tart shells and top each with 1 tablespoon of sweetened whipped cream.

(Any fruit may be used—vary the amount of sugar.)

*'Tis sweet of you to bother, and make nice things for those about you.*

No. 52

## RAISIN SQUARES

Into a sauce pan put 2 tablespoons of sugar—carmelize to a dark brown—add 1¼ cups of water. Let simmer until sugar is disolved—add 1 cup of washed and well drained seedless raisins—⅛ teaspoon of salt—1 tablespoon of butter. Simmer for 10 minutes. Blend together ⅓ cup of sugar with 1 tablespoon corn starch. Stir into the boiling raisins and cook 2 minutes—cool—add 1 teaspoon of vanilla and ¼ teaspoon of lemon flavoring.

Line a shallow pan (12"x9"x2") with pie crust rolled ⅛ inch thick—bringing crust half way up the sides of the pan. Spread on the raisin mixture—cover entire top with pie crust rolled ⅛ inch thick. Press sides together—with a fork prick the entire top crust. Dot with butter. Bake 50 minutes in 375° oven. Cool and cut into squares.

*Pack these in the lunch bag of your favorite person.*

No. 53

## BUTTER CREAM PIE

Line a deep pie tin with pastry crust. Place in the refrigerator one hour to chill.

In a sauce pan—over direct heat carmelize to golden brown 2 tablespoons of sugar—add 2 cups of milk and stir constantly until sugar is disolved—cool slightly.

Mix ⅔ cup of sugar with 3 tablespoons of flour—and 1 tablespoon of corn starch. Beat 2 eggs—add dry ingredients and 2 tablespoons of melted butter.

Combine with the carmelized sugar and milk.

Pour into the chilled pastry shell and bake for 15 minutes in a 425° oven—reduce the heat to 375° and bake 40 minutes longer.

## No. 54

## LEMON CHIFFON PIES

### Of Course You Can Make Them!

Bake over the back of individual pie tins or muffin tins 12 pie shells.

Put on to boil 1½ cups of water—½ cup of lemon juice—1 cup sugar—½ square of butter—⅛ teaspoon of salt.

Mix 4 tablespoon of corn starch in ½ cup of water and stir into the boiling mixture and cook for 2 minutes over direct heat.

Have ready 3 well beaten egg yolks. Pour part of the filling mixture over the egg yolks. Then add this to the balance of the boiling mixture. Take it immediately from the stove and fold the hot filling into 3 egg whites that have been stiffly beaten and blended with ½ cup of sugar—¼ teaspoon of lemon flavoring.

When cool fill into shells and top with whipped cream or meringue.

*For that touch of elegance*

*Where did the hateful idea begin—that*
*ALL cooks are temperamental?*
*Banish the thought! " 'Tis not so, all*
*is well."*

No. 55

## CHICKEN BAKED IN PAN GRAVY

Select a 4 or 5 pound roasting or stewing hen. Clean thoroughly—cut and disjoint. Roll each piece in seasoned flour—made by adding 1 teaspoon of salt—$\frac{1}{8}$ teaspoon of pepper to every 3 tablespoons of flour.

Melt $\frac{1}{2}$ cup of fat (part butter) in frying pan. When hot quickly brown each piece of the chicken on both sides. In the bottom of a casserole slice one medium sized onion. Place chicken in the casserole and make 1 quart of brown gravy with drippings in the pan. Season with salt and pepper—pour over chicken. Cover and bake in 225° oven until tender.

A roasting chicken will cook in 1$\frac{1}{2}$ to 2 hours.

A stewing chicken will require 3$\frac{1}{2}$ to 4$\frac{1}{2}$ hours.

No. 56

## CHICKEN BAKED IN GOLDEN SAUCE

Prepare a four pound chicken (hen)—cover with water add 2 teaspoons of salt, a dash of pepper, 1 large onion. Simmer until tender. Let cool in stock—then remove meat from the bones and cut into large cube pieces.

Add 2 cups diced cooked potatoes—1 cup of peas. Put in well buttered casserole cover with the sauce and bake 40 minutes in 350° oven.

## GOLDEN SAUCE

In sauce pan melt 2 tablespoons of butter—3 tablespoons of chicken fat taken from the chicken stock—blend in 6 tablespoons of flour—and 1½ cups of top milk or thin cream with 2 cups of the chicken stock—1 teaspoon of salt—a dash of pepper. When it begins to thicken, stir in 2 well beaten egg yolks. Cook until thick and smooth.

## No. 57

## ROASTED POULTRY

## CHICKEN OR TURKEY WITH SAGE STUFFING

Thoroughly clean the turkey wash well both inside and out. Chill and wipe dry inside and out. Fill the cavity lightly with the stuffing also the breast and neck skin. Do not pack the stuffing in—leave plenty of room for steam to gather. Sew up the cavity and truss the bird tightly. Rub over with drippings and sprinkle lightly with flour, salt and pepper. Arrange on a trivet in roasting pan and bake 20 minutes to the pound of meat in 300° oven.

## STUFFING

Crumb 2½ quarts of soft bread crumbs discarding all hard crusts. Sprinkle over with 2 teaspoons of salt—¼ teaspoon pepper—4 teaspoons rubbed sage—1 teaspoon thyme.

In a frying pan melt 1 cup of butter or margarine add 1 cup chopped onion—½ cup diced celery. Simmer gently until tender. Toss this mixture through the crumbs until well mixed.

In 1 cup of milk and 1 beaten egg, soak 2 cups of the bread crusts. Add to the stuffing and mix thoroughly.

"We can live without Friends,
We can live without Books,
But civilized men,
CANNOT live without Cooks."

OWEN MEREDITH.

## No. 58

# APPLE PUDDING with BUTTER LEMON SAUCE

Beat 1 egg in mixing bowl—add ½ cup of sugar and beat well—add ¼ cup of buttermilk —1 cup of chopped beef suet—1 teaspoon of vanilla—⅓ teaspoon of salt.

Sift together 1 cup of flour—¼ teaspoon of soda—1½ teaspoons of baking powder—mix with the above ingredients. Add 2 cups of chopped raw apples.

Turn into a buttered bowl—place the bowl in a kettle with water half way up on the bowl. Have a tight fitting lid for the kettle. Steam 1 hour.

## BUTTER LEMON SAUCE

Blend well 4 tablespoons of butter—½ cup of sugar—4 tablespoons flour—add 2 cups of boiling water and cook 1 minute over direct heat. Add ¼ teaspoon of lemon flavoring and the juice and rind of 1 lemon. Add a dash of salt.
Serves eight.

No. 59

## UPSIDE DOWN CARMEL CUSTARD SUPREME

*FOOD—on the luscious side!*

Melt in a heavy sauce pan ½ cup of sugar. Stir until it is a golden brown—pour it into 6 custard cups—sprinkle over with a few broken walnut meats.

Mix together 2 large eggs—slightly beaten with ⅓ cup of sugar mixed well with one level tablespoon of flour and ¼ teaspoon of salt. Add 1½ cups of milk and ½ cup of canned milk—1 teaspoon of vanilla.

Strain into custard cups over the carmelized sugar.

Bake in moderate oven 45 minutes. With the help of a case knife unmold while still warm. Top with whipped cream.

## No. 60

## PLUM ROLLY-POLLY

### with

## CREAM VANILLA SAUCE

Beat 2 eggs until very light—add gradually ½ cup of sugar. Beat together until thick and lemon colored. Add 2 tablespoons of heavy sour cream —¾ cup of chopped beef suet—¼ teaspoon of lemon flavoring.

Sift together and add 1 cup of flour—¼ teaspoon of soda—1½ teaspoon baking powder— ½ teaspoon of salt.

Blend well together and turn out on a well floured baking board. Roll out dough to 1 inch thick—spread with 1 cup of plum jam. Roll up and put into a well buttered bowl. Place bowl in a kettle with water half way up on the bowl. Cover kettle with a tight lid and steam for 1 hour. Serve with cream sauce.

### CREAM SAUCE

Blend ½ square of butter 4 tablespoons flour— ½ cup of sugar—⅛ teaspoon of salt. Add 1½ cups of boiling water. Cook over direct heat for 1 minute—stir constantly. Add ½ cup of light cream and 1 teaspoon of vanilla flavoring.

Serves eight.

No. 61

# CHRISTMAS PUDDING
# (PLUM)

Beat 4 eggs—and gradually beat in $1\frac{1}{2}$ cups of sugar—add $\frac{1}{2}$ cup of buttermilk—$\frac{1}{4}$ cup of maraschino cherry juice—$1\frac{1}{2}$ cup of chopped suet—add 2 cups of bread crumbs—2 cups of seedless raisins—1 cup of chopped almond nuts—1 cup of mixed chopped peel—1 tablespoon of vanilla flavoring.

Sift together 3 times then add—2 cups of flour —1 teaspoon of soda—1 teaspoon of baking powder—1 teaspoon of salt—1 teaspoon of cinnamon—$\frac{1}{2}$ teaspoon of allspice—$\frac{1}{2}$ teaspoon of nutmeg—$\frac{1}{4}$ teaspoon of ginger. Mix well and steam 4 hours. Serve with hard sauce.

## HARD SAUCE

In mixing bowl put 1 square of soft butter— the yolk of 1 egg—1 teaspoon of vanilla flavoring—$\frac{1}{3}$ teaspoon of lemon flavoring—a dash of nutmeg. Beat into this $1\frac{1}{2}$ cups of powdered sugar—beat until creamy and smooth. Set in refridgerator until it hardens. Roll up in wax paper until ready to serve—then slice $\frac{1}{2}$ inch thick and top pudding.

Serves 15.

## No. 62

## CARMEL BAVARIAN

Carmelize in top of double boiler over direct heat ½ cup of sugar until it is a light brown—add 2 cups of milk with ½ cup of canned milk. Put over hot water and bring to a scald and sugar is dissolved.

Soften 1 tablespoon of gelatine in ¼ cup of milk.

Beat 4 egg yolks—add dash of salt—2 tablespoons of sugar—gradually pour scalded milk over egg yolks—return to double boiler and cook until smooth and creamy.

Pour over softened gelatine—stir until gelatine is dissolved. Add 2 teaspoons of vanilla—cool—when it begins to thicken fold in 1 cup of whipped cream and ½ cup of chopped pecan nuts.

Will serve 10.

## No. 63

## APPLES BAKED IN LEMON SAUCE

Peel and core six banana apples. Place in buttered casserole. Into each apple center place 1 teaspoon of washed seedless raisins with a few broken pieces of walnuts. Cover with lemon sauce and bake 45 minutes in 375° oven or until apples are tender. (Prick with a fork to test— cooking time varies.)

## LEMON SAUCE

Bring to a boils 3 cups of water—1 cup of sugar—⅓ cup of lemon juice—¼ teaspoon of salt—½ square of butter. Thicken with ¼ cup of corn starch moistened in ½ cup of water. Add ½ teaspoon of lemon flavoring—1 teaspoon of grated lemon rind—¼ teaspoon of egg yellow coloring.

## No. 64

## PEACH COCKTAIL

*Do you want a change to begin with?*

Place peach halves with cavity side up in a shallow baking pan. In each cavity place 1 teaspoon of brown sugar—a dash of ground cloves —½ teaspoon of butter. Pour just enough cream around the peach halves to cover the bottom of the pan. Bake in 400° oven for 20 minutes. Serve with toasted cheese crackers.

## No. 65

## BROWN BETTY ALA GRANDMOTHER

In a mixing bowl sift 2 cups of flour with 1 cup of sugar—¼ teaspoon of salt—1 teaspoon baking powder.

Rub in 1 cup of butter until it is a very fine mixture—toss through that ¼ cup of chopped candied orange peel.

Butter 9"x12" baking pan—spread in 4 cups of chopped apple mixed thoroughly with ¾ cup of sugar—1 tablespoon of cinnamon—¼ teaspoon of lemon flavoring.

Sprinkle over with the crumb mixture.

Bake in 350° oven 1 hour.

Serve warm with cream—Um, good!

No. 66

## CHOCOLATE SOUFFLE

In the top of the double boiler melt 5 tablespoons of butter—blend in ⅓ cup of flour—add ¼ teaspoon of salt—2 squares of baking chocolate shaved fine ⅔ cup sugar—2 cups of milk. Cook until thick and creamy stirring constantly add 4 well beaten egg yolks. Cook one minute and remove from stove—add ½ cup of chopped nuts—1 tablespoon vanilla—beat one minute—then fold in 4 egg whites beaten stiff with 3 tablespoons of sugar.

Pour into buttered baking dish—place the baking dish in a pan of hot water.

Sprinkle over the souffle ½ cup of chopped nuts. Bake in 325° oven 45 minutes. Serve with whipped cream.

No. 67

## FRESH FRUIT PUDDING

(Peach)

Most any fruits may be used.

Peel and slice 3 cups of fresh peaches. Combine ⅔ cup of sugar with 2 tablespoons of flour. Toss all through the peaches. Add 2 tablespoons of melted butter. Pour into a buttered 9"x12" baking pan.

Cover with cake batter and bake 45 minutes in 375° oven.

## CAKE BATTER

Sift 1 cup of cake flour with 1 teaspoon of baking powder. Beat 2 eggs until very light—add gradually 1 cup of sugar—¼ teaspoon of salt and 1 teaspoon of vanilla flavoring. Heat to scalding ½ cup of cream—1 tablespoon of butter—add to the egg mixture. Beat well—then add the dry ingredients. Beat until smooth—pour over peaches.

## No. 68

## RAISIN SAUCE FOR HAM

Carmelize 2 tablespoons of sugar to a light brown stage—add 2 cups of water and 1 cup of washed and drained raisins (seedless are preferred)—2 tablespoons of butter—1/4 teaspoon of salt—1/8 teaspoon of onion salt—2 tablespoons of sugar—simmer 10 minutes.

Mix 1 tablespoon of corn starch—1 teaspoon of Colman's dry mustard with 1/2 cup of water—stir in and let boil 30 seconds—add 1/4 teaspoon of Worcestershire sauce—1/4 cup of the brown juice from the bottom of the roaster pan in which the ham was baked.

Will make 20 servings.

No. 69

## SAUCES

Tartar Sauce
1 cup mayonnaise
2 tablespoons of lemon juice
½ tablespoon chopped onion (very fine)
1 tablespoon of chopped ripe olives
1 tablespoon of chopped pimiento
2 tablespoons of chopped sweet pickles
Blend thoroughly.

Sweet Mint Sauce for Lamb
1 glass of currant jelly
1 tablespoon of prepared mustard
Place in top of double boiler over hot water.
Beat smooth with egg beater.

Sauce for Sea Food Cocktail
1 cup catsup (Pierces)
4 tablespoons lemon juice
1 tablespoon of Worcestershire sauce
1 tablespoon of horse radish
1 tablespoon of sugar
Blend thoroughly.

## No. 70

## SAUCES

Lemon Sauce
Put on to boil 1 cup of water—add 2 drops of egg yellow coloring. When it comes to a boil, stir in ½ cup of sugar blended with 1 tablespoon of corn starch, ⅛ teaspoon of salt, boil one minute, then add 1 tablespoon of butter with the juice and rind of one lemon. Serve hot on apple cobbler or brown betty.


Carmel Sauce
Brown 4 tablespoons of sugar in sauce pan, add 2 cups of water and ½ cup of sugar, ¼ cup of butter. Bring to a boil—add 3 tablespoons of corn starch moistened in ¼ cup of water. Cook one minute—add 1 teaspoon of vanilla and 1 teaspoon of rum flavoring.

## No. 71

French Dressing

    1 cup of salad oil
    1 cup of catsup (Pierces)
    ¼ teaspoon of paprika
    1 teaspoon of dry mustard
    1 cup of mayonnaise
    ¼ cup of lemon juice
    2 tablespoons of beef steak sauce
    1 teaspoon of sugar
Blend together.

## No. 72

## MIXED RAW GREENS

Salad to you—

## CABBAGE SLAW

Select a hard white head of cabbage. With a sharp knife or cabbage shredder, shred 1 quart of cabbage. Place in the refrigerator to get crisp. (Do not grind or chop cabbage.)

Toss through the cabbage plenty of dressing to make it very moist.

## DRESSING FOR SLAW

Put in a sauce pan 1 cup of white malt vinegar with ¼ cup of water. Bring to boil.

Sift together 3 tablespoons of flour—1 tablespoon of Coleman's dry mustard—6 tablespoons of sugar—⅔ teaspoon of salt. Beat 2 eggs and combine with the dry ingredients. Stir into the boiling vinegar. Let cook 30 seconds. Remove from the stove and with rotary egg beater beat in 3 tablespoons of butter. Pour into a bowl and cool. When cold—fold 1 cup of dressing into 1½ cups of whipped cream. With a fork toss plenty of the dressing over the shredded cabbage to make it very moist.

*What in tarnation will those modern pioneers put together next? Salads, they call them!*

## No. 73

# TOSSED GREENS

### with

### That Famous "Angie Earl Dressing"

Rub the inside of a salad bowl with a cut garlic bud. Shred into the bowl 1 head of lettuce—1 head Romaine—6 leaves of endive—1 cup diced cucumber—3 tablespoons sliced raddish—3 tablespoons of minced green pepper—¼ cup shredded carrot—3 tablespoons of chopped dill pickle.

Marinate thoroughly with 1½ cups of dressing.

## DRESSING

1 cup of Pierces catsup—¼ cup Wesson oil—¼ cup of vinegar (white malt)—1 teaspoon of sugar—1 teaspoon Worcestershire sauce—1 teaspoon of finely chopped onion. Combine all ingredients and blend well with rotary egg beater.

Let dressing stand for several hours in the refrigerator before you marinate the salad greens.

## No. 74

## FROZEN FRUIT SALAD

Whip 1 pint of cream very stiff—add ½ cup of Best Foods mayonnaise—¼ cup of sugar—3 tablespoons of lemon juice—¼ teaspoon of salt. Blend well and place in freezing tray—partly freeze—then add ½ cup of well drained pine-apple—½ cup of chopped walnuts—½ cup of chopped maraschino cherries—1 cup of well drained fruit cocktail. Put back in freezing unit and freeze until solid.

Remove from tray and wrap in several thick-nesses of waxed paper. Place in freezing unit and leave over night or for a day or two to ripen the flavor. Slice and serve on a lettuce leaf. Top with equal parts of whipped cream and mayon-naise blended together. Garnish with grated cheese topped with a maraschino cherry.

*For the guests in best bib and tucker.*

## No. 75

## JELLIED TOMATO AND SHRIMP SALAD

Simmer 20 minutes 2½ cups of canned tomatoes with ½ bay leaf—½ teaspoon of salt—a few grains of cayenne pepper—1 stick of celery —1 small onion—1 tablespoon of lemon juice— one tablespoon of sugar.

Strain and add while hot 1 envelope of plain gelatine softened in ¼ cup of water. Stir until gelatine is thoroughly dissolved. Cool and when it begins to thicken fold in 1 cup of broken pieces of shrimps—½ cup of celery chopped fine—2 tablespoons of chopped green peppers.

Fill crisp lettuce cups—top with mayonnaise— garnish with sliced stuffed olives.

No. 76

## FRUIT SALAD

In the top of a double boiler break three eggs —beat until light—add 5 tablespoons of lemon juice—5 tablespoons of sugar—2 tablespoons of pineapple juice—¼ teaspoon of salt.

Cook until thick and smooth stirring constantly— remove from heat—add 3 tablespoons of butter and cool thoroughly.

Whip 1 cup of cream—fold in 1 cup of diced orange—1 cup of pitted Royal Ann cherries— 2 cups of diced pineapple—2 cups of diced marshmallows. Fold into chilled cooked mixture —turn into ring mold. Let set over night in refrigerator. Unmold and serve with fruit salad dressing—garnish with pecan halves.

## No. 77

## SHAMROCK SALAD

Select 6 slender green peppers—wash and cut slice from the stem end—remove all seeds.

Cream 4 packages of Philadelphia Cream cheese with $\frac{1}{2}$ cup of cream—$\frac{1}{2}$ cup of mayonnaise—3 tablespoons of minced chives—$\frac{1}{4}$ teaspoon of salt. Fill the peppers and place in refridgerator over night.

Prepare 8 lettuce cups—then shred $\frac{1}{4}$ cup of lettuce into each—place 1 tablespoon of mayonnaise on the shredded lettuce. Slice very thin and arrange 3 slices of filled pepper on each bed of lettuce. Garnish with a green cherry and three very small carrot curls.

## No. 78

## TOMATO—PARTY SALAD

Scald and peel 8 firm medium size tomatoes—chill them and scoop out centers with a teaspoon. Sprinkle inside of each with salt—turn upside down on platter. Place in refrigerator to chill.

Dissolve 1 package of lemon jello in 1 cup of hot water—add ½ cup of cold water—3 tablespoons of lemon juice. When it begins to thicken add 1 cup of flaked tuna tossed with 2 tablespoon of mayonnaise—½ cup #2 sifted peas—½ cup of diced celery—1 teaspoon very fine chopped onion and 1 cup of the solid bits of the tomato centers. Fill each tomato with the filling. Set in refrigerator 2 hours. Place each tomato in a lettuce cup—top with mayonnaise and garnish with a slice of hard cooked egg and ripe olive slices.

*Try this on a jaded appetite!*

No. 79

## STUFFED BEETS

Gently boil 12 medium sized beets until very tender. Cool in cold water.

Peel the beets and with a spoon remove the centers. Dice 1 cup of celery—1 cup of the beet centers—¼ cup of cucumber—mince 1 tablespoon of onion—2 tablespoons of green peppers —slice 12 stuffed olives. Combine and moisten with salad dressing. Refill the beets with the mixture. Place each beet in a lettuce cup and garnish with water cress or parsley.

*Everything had to be informal with Pioneer.*

No. 80

## JELLIED FRUIT

Dissolve 1 package of lemon jello in 1 cup of hot pineapple juice—add 1 cup of orange juice and 2 tablespoons of sugar. As it begins to thicken beat to a froth with a rotary egg beater. Then fold in 1 cup of cream whipped with ½ cup of diced pineapple—½ cup of diced orange—½ cup of chopped Brazil nuts.

Place in lettuce cup and top with mayonnaise.

## No. 81

# BRAZIL NUTS

## and

# CUCUMBER JELLIED SALAD

Peel and dice fine 2 cups of dill sized cucumbers. Shred 1 cup of Brazil nuts—toss through them 1 tablespoon of mayonnaise and 2 tablespoons of vinegar.

Let stand while you prepare 2 packages of lime jello—ommitting ½ cup of water from the jello recipe.

When jello begins to thicken fold in the cucuber mixture. Place in a refridgerator until set.

Serve on nests of watercress—top with ½ cup of mayonnaise thinned with ½ cup of whipped cream and 2 tablespoons of lemon juice. Garnish with thin strips of pimiento.

## No. 82

## PINEAPPLE SUPREME SALAD

Dissolve 1 package of lemon jello in 1 cup of boiling water—add 2 tablespoons of lemon juice and $\frac{1}{8}$ teaspoon of egg yellow cake coloring. With a fork cream 1 cup of cottage cheese and combine with 1 cup of grated pineapple—$\frac{1}{2}$ cup of shredded almond nuts—add to jello.

When the jello begin to set—fold in 1 cup of whipped cream. Put in refridgerator until firmly set.

Pile into lettuce cup—top with mayonnaise blended with equal parts of whipped cream and garnish with cherry.

Serves ten.

*Delicious and delicate.*

No. 83

## SCALLOPED ONIONS HUNTER STYLE

A real treat with roast beef dinners!

Peel and soak in salted water 12 medium size white onions.

Drain and cover with hot water—add ½ teaspoon of sugar—½ teaspoon of salt and simmer for 20 minutes. Drain and place in buttered casserole.

Dice and fry 4 slices of bacon. Remove bacon from the pan and add in the pan ⅓ cup of flour —blend well with the fat—add 1 quart of top milk—a dash of pepper—⅔ teaspoon of salt—⅓ teaspoon of onion salt. Cook until smooth and creamy. Add the bacon. Pour over the onions in the casserole—cover the top with buttered bread crumbs. Bake 45 minutes in 325° oven.

Six servings.

*Scalloped onions—Hunter Style, scores a hit every time, with the men friends.*

## No. 84

## COVERED WAGON BAKED BEANS

Wash 2½ cups of navy beans. Soak over night—drain and wash well in fresh water. Cover with water and add 1 pound of salt pork cut into small pieces—1 small garlic bud diced fine. Boil until beans are tender. Add 1 cup of log cabin syrup—1 cup of catsup—and bake in a slow oven—250°—for 2 hours.

Baked Beans (Wanda)
2 c. beans dried          6-8
1/4 lb. bacon
1 1/2 salt ( to taste
1/2 tsp mustard
2 th. molases or more ( Ketchup 2 th. )
1/4 c Br. Sugar
brown 1 onion small.
fry bacon crisp. & crumble
thru beans.

Bake 2 hrs.                    add water

## No. 85

## STUFFED PEPPERS IN TOMATO SAUCE

Select six or eight heavy well shaped peppers —wash and cut slice off the stem end—remove all the seeds.

Combine 1 pound of ground round steak and ½ pound of the best all pork sausage—⅔ cup of minced onion—½ cup rolled oats—1 teaspoon of Coleman's dry mustard (mix the mustard in a little water)—1 teaspoon of salt—1 tablespoon of beefsteak sauce—a dash of pepper—3 tablespoons of catsup—1½ cups of water—1 egg. Mix well.

Fill peppers full and place the top back on. Stand peppers up in a kettle and cover with 1 quart of tomato juice—1 teaspoon of sugar—½ teaspoon of salt—3 tablespoons of butter.

Cover kettle with tight lid and simmer for one hour.

## No. 86

## CORN PUDDING

In a mixing bowl beat 3 eggs well—add $\frac{2}{3}$ cup of canned milk—$\frac{1}{2}$ teaspoon of salt—a dash of pepper—1 tablespoon of chopped fried onion —1 cup of ground bread crumbs—1 can, #2, cream style corn—mix well and turn into well buttered casserole—dot with butter and bake 1 hour in 350° oven.

Serve twelve.

No. 87

## BACON AND POTATOES IN SOUR CREAM GRAVY

Boil in their jackets 16 potatoes (the size of a small orange). Peel and put in a tureen.

Dice and fry eight slices of bacon. Remove bacon to a bowl and fry slowly 1 cup of finely chopped onions in the bacon grease. Fry them until tender but not brown. Return the bacon to the pan, blend well with 3 tablespoons of flour— add 3 cups of top milk or light cream with ¼ cup of lemon juice—1 teaspoon of salt and a dash of pepper. Cook 2 minutes. Pour over the potatoes in the tureen. Garnish with parsley and a dash of paprika.

Serves eight.

No. 88

## STUFFED EGG PLANT

Select a two pound egg plant—wash and cut a slice off the blossom end. With a spoon remove all the center egg plant leaving just a shell to refill.

Boil the egg plant (center) in salted water until tender—turn into a colander and drain well —put back into the kettle and mash with a potato masher.

Prepare 3 cups of soft bread crumbs with 1½ teaspoons of rubbed sage—1 teaspoon of salt— a dash of pepper. Fry ⅔ cup of chopped onion in ½ cup of shortening (part butter). Marinate the bread crumbs combine with the mashed egg plant and 2 beaten eggs.

Fill the egg plant shell. Place in a shallow pan and bake 1 hour in 350° oven.

Or put the stuffed egg plant along side of an oven roast—it makes a fine two-in-one oven job.

No. 89

## CARROTS DRESSED UP FOR A PARTY

Beat 4 egg yolks with 1 tablespoon of flour —add 2 cups of cooked mashed carrots—½ cup of bread crumbs—⅔ teaspoon of salt—a dash of pepper—1 cup of cream whipped. Blend well —then fold in 4 egg whites beaten until they hold a peak.

Pack into 6 well buttered ring molds and place in pan of hot water. Bake in 375° oven for 45 minutes. Unmold and fill the centers with creamed peas.

No. 90

## LIMA BEANS WITH SIDE PORK AND SAGE

Wash well 2 cups of lima beans. Cover with 1 quart of water. Add 2 tablespoons of butter— 3 tablespoons of vinegar—1 teaspoon of salt. Bring to a boil then just simmer for two hours or until the beans are tender. Turn into a casserole.

Put into a frying pan 8 slices of side pork. Sprinkle each slice with a small amount of rubbed garden sage. Place under the broiler and fry a golden brown. Carefully lift the pork slices on to the beans. Cover casserole and return to oven to bake 45 minutes in 300° oven.

Serves eight.

*A homely food pattern—but oh, so good!*

## No. 91

*"How much of this—how little of that."*

The following are bits of precious information that will help you sometime in the future.

## AVERAGE MEASURE FOR USING SALT

Batters and dough:
    1 teaspoon of salt to 4 cups of flour.

Soups and sauces:
    1 teaspoon of salt to each quart.

Ground meat:
    1 teaspoon of salt to each pound.

Roasts:
    ½ teaspoon of salt to the pound.

## AVERAGE WEIGHT OF ONE CUPFULL

    1 cup Milk—½ Pound
    1 cup Sugar—½ Pound
    1 cup Butter—½ Pound
    1 cup All purpose flour—¼ Pound
    1 cup Bread crumbs—2 ounces
    1 cup Corn meal—5 ounces
    1 cup Raisins—6 ounces
    1 cup Rice—½ Pound

## No. 92

## POUNDS

1 Pound of cheese will cut 45 pieces large enough to serve with apple pie.

1 pound of butter creamed will spread 66 sandwiches on two sides.

1 pound of potato chips will serve 30.

1 pound of fresh peas in the pods will serve 2, 3 if you cream them.

1 pound of ground meat will make 12 balls.

1 pound of potatoes before peeling will make 3 large servings.

1 4-pound chicken diced to make salad for 10. If creamed will serve 12 in patty shells.

1 pound of cottage cheese equal 14 tablespoons.

1 pound of ground meat, ham, beef, etc., mixed with ⅔ cup of salad dressing will spread 12 double sandwiches.

## No. 93

## ONE QUART

1 quart of fruit cocktail will make 12 servings.

1 quart of potato salad will serve 7 or 8.

1 quart of salad dressing will top 42 salads.

1 quart of gravy will serve 14 guests.

1 quart of stoned cherries will make 3 pies when sugar and water have been added.

No. 94

## DO YOU KNOW

To fry chopped onions before adding them to recipes enchances the food flavor.

To tenderize baked breads and cake use buttermilk and soda in preference to baking powder and milk—½ teaspoon of soda to 1 cup of buttermilk.

This is truly a pioneer idea.

1½ quarts of raw sliced potatoes—1 small onion and 2 cups of thin white sauce will make scalloped potatoes for 10.

⅔ square of butter will spread 12 double sandwiches.

## No. 95

10 pounds of potatoes will yield 1 gallon of potato salad when diced and mixed with 2 quarts of salad dressing.
Will serve 35.

1 pound of salted nuts will yield 35 servings.

Large mint wafers will count about 50 to the pound.

1 pound of shredded cabbage combined with 1⅓ cup of dressing will yield 7 servings.

1 quart of white sauce to 4 pounds of potatoes will make augrautin potatoes to serve 20.

No. 96

# MY PIONEER MOTHER'S RECIPES

(A few open pages for the buyer to copy in her own favorite "hand-me-downs.")